Wallingford Riegger

Sonatina

for Violin and Piano

Commissioned by the publishers on the occasion of the 25th anniversary of the League of Composers in recognition of its outstanding service to the cause of contemporary music.

ISBN 978-1-4950-0964-8

EXCLUSIVELY DISTRIBUTED BY

HAL•LEONARD®
CORPORATION
7777 W. BLUEMOUND RD. P.O. BOX 13819 MILWAUKEE, WI 53213

www.ebmarks.com
www.halleonard.com

Dedicated to the League of Composers

SONATINA

for Violin and Piano

WALLINGFORD RIEGGER
Op. 39

1

Tempo I°

poco animando

poco animando

Più mosso

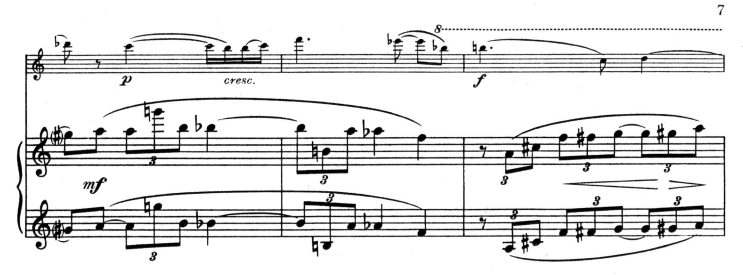

poco slentando sin' al fine

poco slentando sin' al fine

2

Allegro (♩=144)

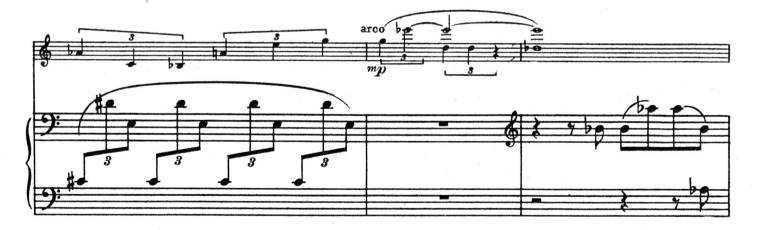

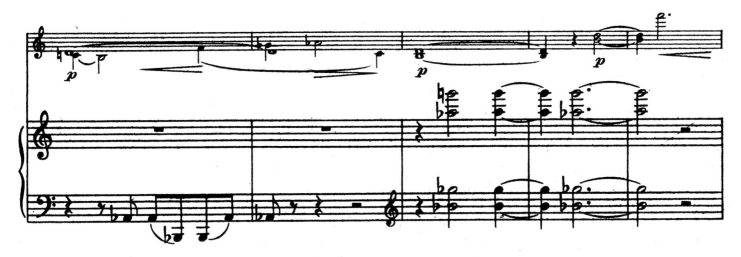

Più mosso (♩ = 80)

Come prima, ma più tranquillo